DANNY SILK

FOUNDATIONS OF
HONOR
STUDY GUIDE
Building a Powerful Community

FIRST EDITION

NEWTYPE Publishing
www.newtypepublishing.com

Cover Design © Yvonne Parks
Interior Design © Renee Evans

ISBN 978-1-942306-09-2
Printed in the United States
www.lovingonpurpose.com

ACKNOWLEDGMENTS

To the Bethel Team,

You've shaped my life in so many ways.
I am forever grateful and humbled to call you friends.

Danny

PUBLISHING TEAM

Allison Armerding—writing & editing
www.allisonarmerding.com

Renée Evans—interior layout design
www.reneeevansdesign.com

NEWTYPE Publishing—printing, marketing, distribution
Ryan Sprenger, CEO
www.newtypepublishing.com

FOUNDATIONS OF
HONOR
STUDY GUIDE

Welcome to the *Foundations of Honor* Study Guide! This study guide is designed to dig deeply into the concepts introduced in the *Foundations of Honor* DVD/Audio Teaching Series and offer insight and guidance as you apply them in your family, business, church, or organization.

Each of the lessons in this study guide examines 3-4 FOUNDATION STONES of honor introduced in the corresponding DVD/Audio session, using the following format:

FOUNDATION STONES:

- SCRIPTURE: Passages relevant to the session's Foundation Stones.

- TEACHING: A brief description and explanation of each Foundation Stone.

- EXAMINE YOUR FOUNDATION: 2-3 questions inviting you to think about where your current beliefs and behavior align and do not align with the Foundation Stone.

- CORE VALUE: A brief statement encapsulating the specific belief about honor contained in this Foundation Stone.

FOUNDATION STORY: These real-life stories from Danny show behavior that aligns, or does not align, with the Foundation Stones.

CULTURAL EFFECTS: This section describes the results that the session's Foundation Stones have on relational culture.

LAYING A SOLID FOUNDATION: This section provides exercises and tools to establish these Foundation Stones in your life, relationships, and community, in the following three areas:

- **STUDY:** Scriptures and other resources for further study and meditation related to the Foundation Stones.

- **PRAY:** Invite God to lead you in incorporating these Foundation Stones.

- **DO:** Ideas for ways to put these Foundation Stones into practice.

HOW TO USE THIS
STUDY GUIDE

Foundations of Honor is designed to be versatile and adaptable for individual and group use. We recommend that you use the following basic format for going through *Foundations of Honor* as a 10-week group study:

WEEKLY MEETING FORMAT FOR SESSIONS 1-9:

- WATCH the DVD Session.

- READ each Foundation Stone.

- DISCUSS the Examine Your Foundation questions (a group facilitator can select the ones most suited for group discussion).

- READ the Story and Cultural Effects.

- DISCUSS Cultural Effects.

- SELECT 1-2 application activities from Lay A Solid Foundation as each week's homework.

SESSION 10:

- Read the Constitution of Honor.

- Discuss the significance and application of each of the commitments listed in the Consitution of Honor in your group and relational environments. (If you choose, you extend this discussion by 1-2 weeks.)

CONTENTS

WHAT IS HONOR?

INTRODUCTION

THE CONTEXT AND DEFINITION OF HONOR

The term *honor* has been around for hundreds of years and has been used in various ways. People associate it with showing respect, holding a personal ethic, protecting a woman's chastity, or being acknowledged for academic achievement. However, none of these definitions refers to the honor you'll be studying in *Foundations of Honor*. In this study, *honor* has a specific definition within a specific context—the context of biblical relationships.

The Bible is primarily an account of relationships. It tells us that a relational, three-person God created a relational humanity in His image, that our relationships with God and one another were damaged through sin, and that God has been carrying out a long-term plan to restore these relationships. Essential to this plan of restoration is the way that God has progressively revealed His design for our relationships through two different covenants.

The **Old Covenant** was a relationship between God and sinners defined through a system of laws, punishments, and sacrifices. In this relationship, God accepted sinners based on their behavior, and fear of punishment was their primary motivation to stay in the relationship. Human authority was directed toward upholding God's laws and punishing lawbreakers.

The **New Covenant** is a relationship between God the Father and His sons and daughters defined by faith, intimacy, and discipleship. The Father accepts sons and daughters based on their faith in Christ's atonement, and love is the primary motivation to stay in the relationship. Human authority is directed towards protecting and nurturing the identity, calling, and connections of God's family members.

God changed His covenantal relationship with us by changing us from condemned sinners to beloved sons and daughters. We have a new identity and nature that require and enable us to relate to Him and to one another in a particular way—the way of honor. In this context, *honor* refers to *the relational values and practices of all who have entered by faith into New Covenant relationships with God and people.*

The purpose of *Foundations of Honor* is to bring definition and clarity to these relational values and practices. Each unit of the study guide will examine several core values of honor—Foundation Stones. We will explore the biblical basis of these core values, examine where our thinking and experience may need correction to align with them more fully, and look at some of the effects that honoring practices should have in relationships, families, and communities.

EXAMINE YOUR FOUNDATION

How have you used and defined the term *honor?*

FOUNDATION STONE #1: FREEDOM

> *It is absolutely clear that God has called you to a free life. Just make sure that you don't use this freedom as an excuse to do whatever you want to do and destroy your freedom. Rather, use your freedom to serve one another in love; that's how freedom grows. For everything we know about God's Word is summed up in a single sentence: Love others as you love yourself. That's an act of true freedom. If you bite and ravage each other, watch out—in no time at all you will be annihilating each other, and where will your precious freedom be then?* GALATIANS 5:13-15 MSG

God is perfect freedom,[1] and He created us in His image to be free. Perfect freedom is *the ability to express God's design for love and relationships.* Though human beings have always tried to find freedom outside of the limits of God's love, doing so has only destroyed their freedom. Honor recognizes that the Father has redeemed His sons and daughters to walk in perfect freedom, and calls them to freedom through empowerment and healthy confrontation.

EXAMINE YOUR FOUNDATION

How is this definition of freedom similar to or different from the way that you have understood freedom?

What is an example of how using freedom outside of the limits of God's love leads to the loss of freedom?

Core Value

Honor calls people to perfect freedom—the ability to express the Father's design for our relationships and reproduce His kingdom of love.

---

[1] see 2 Corinthians 3:17 ESV

FOUNDATION STONE #2: VALUING RELATIONSHIPS

"This is my command: Love one another the way I loved you. This is the very best way to love. Put your life on the line for your friends." JOHN 15:12 MSG

Here's how you tell the difference between God's children and the Devil's children: The one who won't practice righteous ways isn't from God, nor is the one who won't love brother or sister. A simple test. For this is the original message we heard: We should love each other…The way we know we've been transferred from death to life is that we love our brothers and sisters. Anyone who doesn't love is as good as dead. Anyone who hates a brother or sister is a murderer, and you know very well that eternal life and murder don't go together. This is how we've come to understand and experience love: Christ sacrificed his life for us. This is why we ought to live sacrificially for our fellow believers, and not just be out for ourselves. 1 JOHN 3:10-11, 14-16 MSG

We were made in the image of a relational, eternal God, Who has relentlessly pursued the restoration of our eternal relationship with Him, and achieved it through the incredible sacrifice of His Son. Those of us who enter into this restored relationship become *family*—sons and daughters of God, and brothers and sisters to one another. Jesus' primary command is that we love one another as He loved us. We express honor by valuing and treating God-created people and our God-created relationships in the way that God values and treats them.

EXAMINE YOUR FOUNDATION

How would you describe God's value for people and relationships?

What are some of the primary ways God demonstrates His value for people and relationships, which He expects us to imitate?

Core Value

Honor involves valuing, building, and protecting relationships.

FOUNDATION STONE #3: DESTINY

Our Father in heaven,
Hallowed be Your name.
Your kingdom come.
Your will be done
On earth as it is in heaven. MATTHEW 6:9-10 NKJV

Your body has many parts—limbs, organs, cells—but no matter how many parts you can name, you're still one body. It's exactly the same with Christ. By means of his one Spirit, we all said good-bye to our partial and piecemeal lives. We each used to independently call our own shots, but then we entered into a large and integrated life in which he has the final say in everything...I want you to think about how all this makes you more significant, not less. A body isn't just a single part blown up into something huge. It's all the different-but-similar parts arranged and functioning together... But I also want you to think about how this keeps your significance from getting blown up into self-importance. For no matter how significant you are, it is only because of what you are a part of. I CORINTHIANS 12:12, 14, 19 MSG

The New Testament describes us as members of the same body and members of the same family. These metaphors illustrate the truth that each of us has been given unique dreams, talents, and gifts, but all with the same purpose—to serve the mission of our Father to extend His Fatherhood across the globe until His Kingdom comes "on earth as it is in heaven." Honor appreciates the uniqueness of each son and daughter and how that uniqueness contributes to serving the Father's mission. Dishonor occurs when we demand that every son or daughter be the same, when we become jealous or competitive with one another, when we withhold our unique contribution, or when we use it to serve ourselves rather than our Father's mission.

EXAMINE YOUR FOUNDATION

Do you struggle to receive your unique gifts, dreams, and calling? Are you tempted to compare yourself to others or feel jealous?

Do you feel invited and empowered by leaders and people around you to flourish in your calling and gifts?

Core Value

Honor sees how our individual destinies are connected to our common purpose:
"On earth as it is in heaven."

FOUNDATION STORY: "BRITTNEY'S CANDY"

One day, when my daughter, Brittney, was about four years old, her grandmother came to visit her at the group home where we lived and worked with several teenage girls. Brittney's grandmother met her at the front door and held out a roll of Spree candies. "Here's some candy for you," she said, "but you can't have any of your candy until after dinner."

Sheri and I immediately looked at each other with raised eyebrows. We knew there was no way our daughter was not going to eat those candies before dinner. Instead of intervening, however, we sat back and watched Brittney to see what she would do.

Brittney looked at the roll of candy in her hand and walked slowly around the room. Finally, she walked up to one of the teenage girls, took the roll of candies, and broke it in half. She handed half of the candy to the girl and asked, "Can I have some of your candy?"

In that moment, Sheri and I knew we were in trouble. How would we teach this incredibly innovative, powerful, and creative child to use her freedom well? Thankfully, we came across some great tools that introduced us to the core values of honor. Instead of shutting down Brittney's freedom out of fear, we were able to guide her towards successfully managing her freedom to protect and strengthen relationships.

CULTURAL EFFECTS
FREEDOM:

- Leaders have a goal of increasing the freedom of everyone in the environment. The relationship between leaders and followers is mutually empowering.

- People are accountable to confront behavior that violates freedom and love in themselves and others.

RELATIONSHIPS:

- Anxiety decreases and cooperation increases because people know that they are more valuable than any particular task or mission.

- Marriages, families, partnerships, and teams thrive and endure.

DESTINY:

- People acknowledge the corporate vision and mission to demonstrate the Father's heart and allow people to flourish as beloved sons and daughters.

- People are extremely passionate, productive, creative, and cooperative, and a wide diversity of gifts, talents, and dreams gets to be expressed and realized.

REFLECT & DISCUSS:

Do you see these cultural effects in your relational environment(s)? Explain.

"If people knew who God made them to be, they would never want to be someone else."

BILL JOHNSON

LAY A SOLID FOUNDATION

STUDY

- Freedom: Romans 8:21, Galatians 5:13-23

- Relationships: John 15:9-14, 1 John 3:14-18

- Destiny: Galatians 6:4-6 (MSG)

PRAY

- Scripture declares, "Where the Spirit of the Lord is, there is freedom" (2 Corinthians 3:17 ESV). Invite the Holy Spirit to reveal any areas where you need greater freedom from sin and greater freedom to love. Write down what you hear and invite the Spirit into those areas with His freedom.

- Ask the Lord to show you any place where honor needs to be restored or strengthened in your relationships, and to impart His value for each person in your life.

- Ask the Lord to continue to reveal His Father's heart toward you and toward others and remove any orphan thinking and behavior in your life.

DO

- Write out a personal statement describing how and where you want to grow in freedom, value for relationships, and greater alignment with personal and corporate destiny through Foundations of Honor and beyond.

CULTIVATING AN ABUNDANCE MINDSET

SESSION 2

CULTIVATING AN ABUNDANCE MINDSET

FOUNDATION STONE #4: THE FATHER'S ABUNDANCE

> *He who did not spare His own Son, but delivered Him up for us all, how shall He not with Him also freely give us all things?* ROMANS 8:3
>
> *Indeed I have all and abound… And my God shall supply all your need according to His riches in glory by Christ Jesus.* PHILIPPIANS 4:18, 20
>
> *The thief does not come except to steal, and to kill, and to destroy. I have come that they may have life, and that they may have it more abundantly.* JOHN 10:10

2 Peter 1:3

The Father has appointed His sons and daughters as heirs of the limitless abundance of His Kingdom. All the love, joy, hope, wisdom, revelation, courage, healing, and grace we could ever need to reach our potential as lovers of God and people is ours. Stepping towards our Father and His mind-boggling promises requires us to replace a lack mindset with an abundance mindset. We honor the Father by joyfully asking for and receiving His "more than enough" for our lives, and by pouring out the resources of our lives to those around us. Leaders who lead with honor model and impart an abundance mentality by offering resources, opportunities, and guidance to help people dream, grow, and expand their horizons of hope and possibility.

EXAMINE YOUR FOUNDATION

Are there areas where you struggle to believe that there's not enough—love, healing, affection, hope, power, provision, etc.—for you?

Who is someone in your life who demonstrates an abundance mindset, and how does he/she demonstrate it?

Core Value

People of honor carry an abundance mindset based on the Father's heart to supply every son and daughter with the resources, opportunities, and wisdom they need to flourish, succeed, and overflow with blessing to others.

FOUNDATION STONE #5: ABUNDANCE AND AUTHORITY

"Therefore do not worry, saying, 'What shall we eat?' or 'What shall we drink?' or 'What shall we wear?' For after all these things the Gentiles seek. For your heavenly Father knows that you need all these things. But seek first the kingdom of God and His righteousness, and all these things shall be added to you. MATTHEW 6:31-33

> *Then Jesus answered and said to them, "Most assuredly, I say to you, the Son can do nothing of Himself, but what He sees the Father do; for whatever He does, the Son also does in like manner. For the Father loves the Son, and shows Him all things that He Himself does; and He will show Him greater works than these, that you may marvel."* JOHN 5:19-20

Jesus demonstrated His Father's "more than enough" for every situation or person He encountered, but He also made it clear that abundance flowed through His life because He was fully submitted to the Father's will. As sons and daughters, our abundance mentality must be connected with the value of honoring and aligning ourselves with the Father's mission and the leaders He has raised up to equip us to fulfill that mission.

Some people mistakenly think that honor either enforces a hierarchical authority structure in relationships, or else flattens and/or removes authority altogether (plural leadership). But honoring environments have powerful leaders that lead, empower, and equip people just as Jesus did. People of honor carry a value of submitting (protecting relationship out of love) and staying accountable to godly leaders, fathers, and mothers in their lives.

EXAMINE YOUR FOUNDATION

Are you accountable to godly authority in your life? How has this blessed you?

What qualities and behavior should you look for in order to determine whether someone can be entrusted with greater resources and authority?

Core Value

While the resources of the Father's house are unlimited, they flow to and through us as we become fully aligned with His heart and His mission, and with the leaders He has called to equip us to fulfill that mission.

FOUNDATION STONE #6: GENEROSITY

> *The world of the generous gets larger and larger;*
> *the world of the stingy gets smaller and smaller.*
> *The one who blesses others is abundantly blessed;*
> *those who help others are helped.* PROVERBS 11:24-35 MSG
>
> *God loves it when the giver delights in the giving. God can pour on the blessings in astonishing ways so that you're ready for anything and everything, more than just ready to do what needs to be done... This most generous God who gives seed to the farmer that becomes bread for your meals is more than extravagant with you. He gives you something you can then give away, which grows into full-formed lives, robust in God, wealthy in every way, so that you can be generous in every way, producing with us great praise to God.* 2 CORINTHIANS 9:7B-8, 10-11 MSG

The English word *generous* originally meant "of noble birth."[2] Generosity has always been an expression of nobility, and it should be a defining quality of the Father's sons and daughters. When we imitate the generosity of our Father, we reveal His heart and bring Him glory and honor. We also honor those He has asked us to bless. The Bible is clear that generosity is a mutual blessing to the giver and the receiver.

---

[2] "generous," Online Etymology Dictionary, http://www.etymonline.com/index.php?term=generous&allowed_in_frame=0 (accessed June 9, 2015).

EXAMINE YOUR FOUNDATION

Who has demonstrated generosity in your life and in what ways?

joy to glorify God

How has this generosity influenced you?

Core Value

*Generosity is an essential joy, privilege,
and responsibility for people of honor.*

FOUNDATION STORY: "GOD'S DREAMS ARE BIGGER"

As a young man, I worked as a butcher in a grocery store in Weaverville, CA a town of 3,000. Though I was a new believer, God had already planted a conviction in my heart that I was meant to do something great for the Kingdom. While cutting meat and serving customers, I dreamt about what my life could look like in the future. The most extravagant thing my imagination could invent was that I would one day buy the grocery store where I worked and turn it into a vehicle to serve the poor in Weaverville.

I'm going to be the best grocery store owner in this town, I thought. *Nothing is impossible.*

Thirty years later, my life looks nothing like what I used to imagine. I now travel the world and minister to hundreds of thousands of people. I am living a dream far beyond anything I could have even comprehended. It's not the dream I had for myself; it's the dream my Father had for me. Sometimes I wonder what would have happened if God had let me be contained by my own dreams. I'm so thankful that He led me outside the limited box of my imagination and showed me the abundance He had for me as His son. When we choose to honor Him by trusting Him with our hopes and dreams, He will generously entrust us with His incredible dreams for us.

CULTURAL EFFECTS
ABUNDANCE MENTALITY:

- People are expected and empowered to run after their God-given calling and dreams, confident that all they need will be supplied.

- Leaders work to give people opportunities and to put them in roles where they will excel and grow.

AUTHORITY:

- People look for opportunities to serve because they love their leaders and believe in the mission.

- Leaders work themselves out of a job by raising people up around them to be partners.

GENEROSITY:

- People enjoy giving and give extravagantly.
- People don't throw money at problems; they invest in people.

REFLECT & DISCUSS:

Do you see these cultural effects in your relational environment(s)? Explain.

LAY A SOLID FOUNDATION

STUDY

- Abundance: Luke 11:9-13, Matthew 5:42-45

- Authority: Ephesians 6:1-4

- Generosity: Consider how these different translations render Isaiah 32:8, and meditate on the connection between being generous, being noble, and being honorable:

  But a generous man devises generous things,
  And by generosity he shall stand. (NKJV)

  But he who is noble plans noble things,
  and on noble things he stands. (ESV)

  An honorable man makes honorable plans;
  his honorable character gives him security. (NET)

- Recommended Listening: "Expectation and Expectancy" by Danny Silk, available online at the Bethel Store: https://shop.ibethel.org/products/expectation-and-expectancy

PRAY

- Invite the Lord to show you any area of your life where you believe there isn't enough, and ask Him to align your thinking and faith with the truth of His abundance. Ask for greater faith to ask, receive, and give in ways that befit a true son or daughter.

- Pray for every leader you know to encounter, communicate, and demonstrate the Father's heart in greater measure. Pray for a heart of honor to obey and stay accountable to the leaders God has placed in your life, as unto Him.

- Ask God for increased wisdom in "devising generous things," and increased joy and cheerfulness in giving.

DO

- Part of developing your abundance mentality is exercising your imagination to dream bigger. Write down your Top 10 dreams and look for how you can better align your imagination with the reality of your Father's abundance.

- Choose one or two of the people you are fathering, mothering, leading, or influencing and give them an encouraging word about how the Father sees them or how they are honoring the Father through their lives.

- Choose a person, family, group, or organization you would like to honor with a gift of some kind this year—time, money, service, etc. Ask God for a strategy for what and when to give, and enjoy the process of planning, saving, and giving!

CONFRONTATION, PART I—THE NEED FOR FEEDBACK

SESSION 3

CONFRONTATION, PART I—THE NEED FOR FEEDBACK

FOUNDATION STONE #7: THE NEED FOR CONFRONTATION

"If a fellow believer hurts you, go and tell him—work it out between the two of you. If he listens, you've made a friend. If he won't listen, take one or two others along so that the presence of witnesses will keep things honest, and try again. If he still won't listen, tell the church. If he won't listen to the church, you'll have to start over from scratch, confront him with the need for repentance, and offer again God's forgiving love." MATTHEW 18:15-17 MSG

A quiet rebuke to a person of good sense
does more than a whack on the head of a fool. PROVERBS 17:10 MSG

The term *confrontation* triggers anxiety for many people simply because the experience of confrontation often involves vulnerability, stress, and pain. Yet healthy confrontation is essential to preserving relational connections. In every kind of relationship—wherever there are people—various types of conflict are bound to arise. Unresolved conflict rapidly erodes safety and connection in relationships. People who avoid confrontation end up with unhealthy, low-trust, fragile relationships. Healthy confrontation approaches relational conflict as medicine approaches injury and illness—preventing conflict is our first priority, followed by a proactive plan to confront and resolve conflict when it arises.

EXAMINE YOUR FOUNDATION

Has your experience confronting people and/or being confronted been positive or negative? Explain.

_____

_____

_____

_____

_____

What would you say is essential to resolving relational conflict?

_____

_____

_____

_____

_____

Core Value

*People of honor are prepared to confront behavior
that threatens the health of relational connections.*

FOUNDATION STONE #8: A VALUE FOR FEEDBACK

So let's agree to use all our energy in getting along with each other. Help others with encouraging words; don't drag them down by finding fault…May our dependably steady and warmly personal God develop maturity in you so that you get along with each other as well as Jesus gets along with us all. Then we'll be a choir—not our voices only, but our very lives singing in harmony in a stunning anthem to the God and Father of our Master Jesus! ROMANS 14:19, 15:5-6 MSG

Don't pick on people, jump on their failures, criticize their faults— unless, of course, you want the same treatment. That critical spirit has a way of boomeranging. It's easy to see a smudge on your neighbor's face and be oblivious to the ugly sneer on your own. Do you have the nerve to say, 'Let me wash your face for you,' when your own face is distorted by contempt? It's this whole traveling road-show mentality all over again, playing a holier-than-thou part instead of just living your part. Wipe that ugly sneer off your own face, and you might be fit to offer a washcloth to your neighbor. Matthew 7:1-5 MSG

Cultivating the skill of giving and receiving feedback is one of the most important keys to *preventing* relational conflict. If strengthening and preserving healthy relational connections is our first priority, then we must courageously pursue awareness of how the people around us are experiencing us. We all need feedback that affirms what we are doing well and identifies areas where we can grow or improve. We honor the people around us when we allow them to speak into our lives, and they honor us when they give us feedback that will enable us to "happen" more effectively in our lives and relationships. All honoring feedback, especially correction, must be grounded in the Father's heart that enables us to see one another, even as we make messes, as beloved sons or daughters who are destined and called to look just like Jesus.

EXAMINE YOUR FOUNDATION

What is the most valuable feedback you've ever received? How did you respond to it?

EXAMINE YOUR FOUNDATION

What is the worst feedback you've ever received? How did you respond to it?

To whom are you giving feedback in life? Do you feel like your feedback aligns with the Father's heart for these people?

Core Value

As people of honor, we highly value giving and receiving feedback to create awareness of how others are experiencing us, and we are experiencing others.

FOUNDATION STONE #9: A SAFE PLACE

What this adds up to, then, is this: no more lies, no more pretense. Tell your neighbor the truth. In Christ's body we're all connected to each other, after all. When you lie to others, you end up lying to yourself…Watch the way you talk. Let nothing foul or dirty come out of your mouth. Say only what helps, each word a gift. Don't grieve God. Don't break his heart. His Holy Spirit, moving and breathing in you, is the most intimate part of your life, making you fit for himself. Don't take such a gift for granted. Make a clean break with all cutting, backbiting, profane talk. Be gentle with one another, sensitive. Forgive one another as quickly and thoroughly as God in Christ forgave you.
EPHESIANS 4:25, 29-32 MSG

The goal of exchanging feedback is to give one another good information about how we are affecting each other in order to *strengthen our relational connections*. This exchange of truth will only be successful in a safe place, which we create by communicating in kind, respectful ways. Here are some crucial guidelines for how to give and receive feedback that is safe, respectful, and truthful:

let people to know what is going inside of you. Its ok to express our needs

When giving feedback:

- Understand that it is your responsibility to give the other person good information about what is going on inside you. Do not expect the person to read your mind.

- Address how you are experiencing the person's behavior, not what you think about their motives or character.

- Use "hero sandwiches"—send twice as much positive feedback as constructive feedback.

- Use "I messages" to communicate the truth about your thoughts, feelings, and needs. The basic structure of an "I message" is: "When this happened, I felt (emotion). I need to feel (emotion)."

- Trust the other person to care about your feelings and needs and be willing to adjust to protect your connection.

When receiving feedback:

- Listen in order to *understand* what the other person is telling you. You can't do anything productive until you understand what he or she is trying to say.

- Use reflective listening in order to gain understanding. "Let me see if I understand…"

- Listen to identify the *need* the other person is trying to express to you. Identifying the need will allow you to create a strategy for adjusting to meet that need and strengthen or heal the relationship.

EXAMINE YOUR FOUNDATION

Do you expect people to know what you're thinking and feeling without communicating it?

What makes you feel safe when receiving feedback?

Core Value

People of honor create a safe place to give and receive feedback.

FOUNDATION STONE #10: ADJUSTING TO MEET NEEDS

Get along among yourselves, each of you doing your part…Be patient with each person, attentive to individual needs. And be careful that when you get on each other's nerves you don't snap at each other. Look for the best in each other, and always do your best to bring it out. I THESSALONIANS 5:13, 15 MSG

Exposing your needs in a relationship and adjusting to meet the other person's needs are both expressions of honor. Our value for people and relationships must include the willingness to adjust to people who may have very different needs than we do.

The "I message" is specifically designed to identify what a person is needing to experience in a relationship. Here are some examples of "I messages":

- "When you asked me to do that for you, but didn't explain how to do it, I felt anxious and frustrated. I want to help, but I *need* good information and clarity so I can be successful."

- "When you are consistently late for our appointments, I feel disrespected and devalued. I *need* to feel more value from you in our relationship."

- "I feel scared when you speak to me in a raised voice. I want to hear what you have to say, but I *need* to be able to feel safe with you to do that."

Learning to use the "I message" will help you gain greater skill and discernment both in communicating and listening for vital information about what's going on inside you and others. Once the need has been clearly identified, then you can make a plan for how to adjust.

EXAMINE YOUR FOUNDATION

Do you communicate what you need in relationships? What are some needs that have been difficult for you to communicate?

EXAMINE YOUR FOUNDATION

Has someone expressed a need in your relationship that you don't easily relate to? Were you willing to adjust to the other person?

Core Value

People of honor care about meeting the needs of the other person in the relationship and will adjust in order to do so.

FOUNDATION STORY: "THE UNSCHEDULED MEETING"

One day after teaching in the School of Ministry, I returned to my office and found Dann Farrelly and Paul Manwaring waiting there for me.

"Hey, are we having a meeting?" I asked, wondering if I had missed seeing it on my calendar.

Dann got up and closed my door. I immediately understood that we *were* having a meeting, just not one that we had previously scheduled.

After Dann sat down, he looked at me and said, "Hey, I was wondering if you have some hurt or bitterness in your heart towards Kris Vallotton."

I pondered this for a moment, then answered honestly, "Not that I know of. I feel good towards him."

Paul spoke up. "Today during lunch, the way the two of you were talking to each other scared me. I've seen you two disconnected before, and it's not fun for any of us."

I promised the two of them that I would go to Kris and make sure we were on good terms. I left my office, found Kris, and asked him if he thought our conversation had felt disrespectful or dishonoring.

"Hmm…" Kris frowned. "No, I thought we were having a great conversation."

"So did I," I agreed. "But we scared Dann and Paul with our intensity, and maybe scared the rest of the team, so I will find them and let them know everything is okay. Thanks."

I managed to track down Dann and Paul a little later that day and tell them what Kris had said. "I'm very sorry that we scared you," I apologized. "I'll adjust."

They both thanked me for letting them be powerful enough in our relationship to give me feedback and for showing them that I would adjust to project our relationship.

CULTURAL EFFECTS
CONFRONTATION:

- People grow increasingly powerful—courageous, self-controlled, and responsible—as they protect the quality of their lives and relationships.

- People feel accepted, loved, known, and understood, and overcome past wounds and deficits, as they work through conflict toward understanding and greater connection.

FEEDBACK:

- Conflict is minimal because good feedback has taught people how to appreciate and adjust to one another.

- Every single person gets and gives feedback on a regular basis.

SAFE PLACE:

- People are freed from issues because they don't have to hide their deepest fears and hurts.

- Relationships are strengthened as people experience being heard and valued.

MEETING NEEDS:

- Relationships grow in intimacy and trust because they tangibly experience sacrificial love.

- Individuals grow in their ability to love and to appreciate people who are different than they are.

REFLECT & DISCUSS:

Do you see these cultural effects in your relational environment(s)? Explain.

LAY A SOLID FOUNDATION

STUDY

- Confrontation: Matthew 5:22-24

- Feedback: Proverbs 1:7-8

- Safe Place: Proverbs 11:14, 24:6

- Meeting Needs: John 13:3-10

- Recommended Listening: "Brave Communication" by Dann Farrelly, available online at the Bethel Store: https://shop.ibethel.org/products/brave-communication

PRAY

- Ask God to heal you from any fear of confrontation. Invite Him to give you wisdom, courage, and grace to forgive offenses and to confront those that do need to be addressed.

- Pray the prayer of David inviting God's feedback in your life:

  Investigate my life, O God,
  find out everything about me;
  Cross-examine and test me,
  get a clear picture of what I'm about;
  See for yourself whether I've done anything wrong—
  then guide me on the road to eternal life. (Psalm 139:23-24 MSG)

- Ask God for grace to speak the truth in love and build greater trust and intimacy in your relationships, and for His heart to care about and adjust to meet the needs of those He has placed in your life.

DO

- If you identified any area of your life where you feel you need better feedback, seek it out. Pay attention to the people in your life this week and look for occasions to give positive feedback.

- Repent for any harsh, critical words that you have spoken and apologize if necessary. If you have any relational connection that feels distant or damaged, make a plan to strengthen your connection.

- Ask someone close to you this week, "What do you need from me? How can I serve you?"

- Build the following into your life:

  a. People who are welcome to give you feedback every day.

  b. A habit of asking people around you, "How are you experiencing me? Do you have any feedback for me?"

CONFRONTATION, PART II—SKILLS FOR SUCCESS

SESSION 4

CONFRONTATION, PART II—SKILLS FOR SUCCESS

FOUNDATION STONE #11: HUMILITY

> *Fear of the LORD teaches wisdom;*
> *humility precedes honor* PROVERBS 15:33 ESV
>
> *I therefore, a prisoner for the Lord, urge you to walk in a manner worthy of the calling to which you have been called, with all humility and gentleness, with patience, bearing with one another in love, eager to maintain the unity of the Spirit in the bond of peace.* EPHESIANS 4:1-3 ESV

Humility is the posture of love and honor—the posture of pouring yourself out to serve others and treating them as more important than yourself. Valuing feedback, adjusting to needs, forgiving quickly, and being slow to take offense express humility. Humility is critical to successful confrontation. Before we attempt to confront someone, some of the things we should honestly ask ourselves include:

1) Have I truly forgiven this person from my heart?

2) Do I have compassion and love for them as a fellow brother or sister?

3) Is my heart's desire to serve this person?

4) Have I identified the emotions and needs I hope to communicate?

5) What are some "I messages" that express what I need to say?

6) Have I consulted someone I am accountable to who can check to see if my heart is right?

When being confronted, we show humility by listening well to what the other person is trying to communicate, putting their needs and concerns before our own, and serving them by adjusting to resolve the issue.

EXAMINE YOUR FOUNDATION

Do you know how the people around you experience you?

Do you know what the people around you need from you?

What adjustments have you made to address those needs?

Core Value

People of honor walk in humility.
Humility is essential to successful confrontation.

FOUNDATION STONE #12: ASKING GOOD QUESTIONS

Now prepare yourself like a man,
I will question you, and you shall answer Me JOB 38:3

Brethren, if a man is overtaken in any trespass, you who are spiritual restore such a one in a spirit of gentleness, considering yourself lest you also be tempted. GALATIANS 6:1

Counsel in the heart of man is like deep water,
But a man of understanding will draw it out. PROVERBS 20:5

The first goal in a confrontation is to understand what has been causing conflict in a relationship or relational environment—not only on the level of behavior, but also on the level of beliefs, emotions, and needs. When formulated and asked by a skilled listener operating in humility and gentleness, powerful questions create a safe place for people to tell the truth about what is going on inside of them so that the "problem" can be accurately identified. They also empower people to achieve the second goal of a confrontation—creating an effective solution for resolving the conflict and its underlying issues.

EXAMINE YOUR FOUNDATION

Why do questions help lower anxiety, while statements tend to increase defensiveness?

EXAMINE YOUR FOUNDATION

What kinds of questions have created a safe place for you to open up about what's going on inside you?

_____

_____

_____

_____

_____

What was an occasion where you identified a "broken spot" responsible for patterns of behavior that were hurting yourself and your relational connections? What enabled you to see and identify this broken place?

_____

_____

_____

_____

_____

Core Value

Asking good questions in a confrontation creates a safe place to find the core problem(s) needing resolution.

FOUNDATION STONE #13: BUILDING SOLUTIONS

He who disdains instruction despises his own soul,
But he who heeds rebuke gets understanding. PROVERBS 15:32

He who gets wisdom loves his own soul;
He who keeps understanding will find good. PROVERBS 19:8

Every problem must have an owner, and the owner is the best person to fix the problem. Once the person being confronted has identified and owned their problem (or part of the problem) that is causing conflict, the next step in the confrontation is to help them build a solution to their own problem. A solution includes the following:

1) A plan to apologize and make repairs ("clean up the mess") with every person affected by the conflict.

2) A mutually understood and approved list of adjustments necessary to prevent future conflict.

3) A plan for how to make these adjustments successfully. Accountability is an essential part of this plan.

As you help another person build a solution to his/her problem, you send the message that he/she is a powerful son or daughter who gets to rise up in this moment, cheered on by a Father and family who love them and are *for* them, and be more than a conqueror over the things that are threatening their identity, freedom, and connections.

EXAMINE YOUR FOUNDATION

Have you tried to help someone solve a problem that they didn't "own"? How did that work out?

EXAMINE YOUR FOUNDATION

Have you had an experience when someone else helped show you the truth about a problem in your life? How did you respond to them?

_____

_____

_____

_____

_____

Do you have an example of a successful confrontation? What made it successful?

_____

_____

_____

_____

_____

Core Value

The best person to fix a problem is its owner.
Confrontation empowers people to own their problems and collaborate in creating powerful solutions to them.

FOUNDATION STORY: "ANDY'S EMAIL"

Andy and Janine Mason are gifted leaders with whom I have had the honor of partnering in various capacities. Some years ago, I helped Andy launch the Global Transformation Institute (GTI), a coaching and training resource for leaders in the marketplace. I perceived my role with GTI as a facilitator and advisor supporting Andy in the top leadership position. However, one day a scheduling conflict revealed that Andy's perception and my perception of our roles were not on the same page. An email from Andy landed in my inbox and asked me some direct and vulnerable questions:

Hi Danny,

…I felt disappointed that you were not going to be at what I believed to be a GTI event, and even more so to hear it from [someone besides you]. I appreciate you obviously trust us with this, but feel abandoned in the battlefield with no communication from headquarters. I'm not sure whether GTI is yours or 'ours,' or if you are nursing it along until you can offload it onto me. This is not fun. I feel like you have given me a key to the house (freedom and empowerment) but I still need direction and guidance to find my way around.

Looking forward to hearing how you see this.

Peace to your house,
Andy Mason

I immediately wrote back:

Andy,

I'm sorry that you found out this way…Poor communication on my part. I did see [GTI] as something you and Janine would primarily carry and didn't think I was creating a problem. I'm not wanting you to feel abandoned, ever. I am very much a partner and very sorry if you're not feeling that. I have no intention of off-loading GTI onto you, but I do expect your leadership role to increase. We can talk more about this if you need to. I love you and value our partnership. Again, I'm sorry this came down this way. I understand how you would feel shocked and even hurt by my behavior. Please forgive me.

Peace,
Danny
PS: good feedback!

Andy responded a short time later:

Thanks so much for your response, Danny. I'd already forgiven you :) I'm also learning to communicate more — how I feel, what I need…My default has been suppression and silence, and that doesn't build intimacy or trust (or health). Thanks for hearing and validating what I feel and not just pointing out my own insecurities and fears.

Relationship is really important to me. I don't want to just accomplish something great with GTI. I want to build strong relationships on the way. Anthony West said something to me the other day that challenged my alignment: "Success in the kingdom is not about accomplishment, but about relationship." I don't want to just build my own thing or build something for you. I want to build WITH you.

I love you,

Andy

Humility looks like two powerful people who are willing to be vulnerable and to adjust to meet one another's needs. I'm so thankful for Andy and how he demonstrated honoring feedback and confrontation—not only for the sake of our relationship, but for the sake of all the people our relationship touches.

CULTURAL EFFECTS

HUMILITY:

- Fear of confrontation is low because everyone knows it will be done in gentleness, and there is hope for a successful resolution.

- Willingness to adjust is high because the culture of serving one another assures everyone that their needs will be met.

POWERFUL QUESTIONS:

- Good questions send a message of respect that lowers anxiety, invites people into a safe space to be known, and affirms the value of all people involved in the confrontation.

- Good questions bring the relief of finally discovering the truth of what has been going on, and hope that a solution can be found for it.

BUILDING SOLUTIONS:

- People are empowered to take responsibility for their own issues.

- People gain greater wisdom about how they're affecting their environment and the root causes of their behavior.

REFLECT & DISCUSS:

Do you see these cultural effects in your relational environment(s)? Explain.

LAY A SOLID FOUNDATION

STUDY

- Humility: Matthew 11:29.

- Powerful Questions: Mark 10:46-52. What was the purpose of Jesus' powerful question in this encounter?

- Solving Problems: Hebrews 12:1-17. How does the Lord's discipline and correction in our lives enable us to take responsibility for our own problems and, with His grace, find effective solutions to them?

PRAY

- Ask Jesus to unveil the beauty of His humility and increase your ability to serve others.

- Ask God for increased wisdom and understanding to ask powerful questions in confrontation.

- Pray for God to give you hope and faith for any relational issue that seems hopeless. Invite the Holy Spirit to lead you through any prayers of forgiveness and intercession for the person with whom you are struggling to connect.

DO

- If there's someone in your life who is struggling in some areas or from whom you feel disconnected, ask how you can serve or connect with that person.

CONFRONTATION, PART III—RESULTS

SESSION 5

CONFRONTATION, PART III—RESULTS

FOUNDATION STONE #14: STRONGER PEOPLE

> *For the word of God is living and powerful, and sharper than any two-edged sword, piercing even to the division of soul and spirit, and of joints and marrow, and is a discerner of the thoughts and intents of the heart.* HEBREWS 4:12

Every aspect of confrontation creates opportunities for people to grow and to become more powerful in their ability to love God and people. Being vulnerable about the heart issues connected to conflict is a powerful choice. The process of exposing the truth of these heart issues yields invaluable wisdom and awareness about individual needs, emotions, behavior styles, and wounds, which enable people to step into greater freedom and healing. The courageous choice to step toward one another in the midst of disconnection strengthens people's commitment to being people of honor and building honoring relationships. Successful confrontation increases the level of power, freedom, and honor in individual lives.

EXAMINE YOUR FOUNDATION

How has confrontation increased your self-awareness and understanding of your needs, emotions, behavior style, and wounds?

_____
_____
_____
_____
_____

How has confrontation—either confronting or being confronted—required you to be more powerful?

_____
_____
_____
_____
_____

Core Value

A successful confrontation enables people to grow in vulnerability, self-awareness, wisdom, love, courage, freedom, and commitment to honor.

FOUNDATION STONE #15: STRONGER CONNECTIONS

It's better to have a partner than go it alone.
Share the work, share the wealth.
And if one falls down, the other helps,
But if there's no one to help, tough!
Two in a bed warm each other.
Alone, you shiver all night.
By yourself you're unprotected.
With a friend you can face the worst.
Can you round up a third?
A three-stranded rope isn't easily snapped. ECCLESIASTES 4:9-12 MSG

Successful confrontation will always strengthen relational connections. Confrontation not only helps to identify and resolve issues causing disconnection; it enables people to love one another more skillfully, which prevents conflict and makes connections more conflict-resilient. The process of identifying one another's needs and working together to meet them will build the deepest level of intimacy in relationships. This is God's design for relationships—mutual submission, mutual love. Confrontation helps us to align with, and ultimately experience, this design.

EXAMINE YOUR FOUNDATION

How has confrontation helped to uncover unmet needs in a conflict?

EXAMINE YOUR FOUNDATION

How has confrontation helped lead to stronger connections in your relationships?

Core Value

*A successful confrontation strengthens relational connections
by resolving harmful conflict
and by identifying ways to meet people's needs more effectively.*

FOUNDATION STONE #16: WHEN CONFRONTATION DOESN'T GO WELL

Then Peter came to Him and said, "Lord, how often shall my brother sin against me, and I forgive him? Up to seven times?" Jesus said to him, "I do not say to you, up to seven times, but up to seventy times seven." MATTHEW 18:21-22

You did everything you could to set up a successful confrontation. You prayed and forgave from your heart. You asked respectful questions and communicated the issues as clearly and humbly as you could. You took responsibility for your part and made your appeal to fix the issue and reconcile the relationship. You brought in a mediator to keep things safe and accountable. You followed the biblical process of successive confrontations. Despite all this, the other person refused to adjust and repair your connection. What now?

- Wait and Pray: Sometimes people will process the confrontation, come to terms with the issues, and decide to work on reconciliation. Pray for grace to be patient and leave room for this change of heart.

- Grieve: This person has broken your heart. While you can still hold on to hope that they will have a change of heart, they have caused a painful loss that has put you in a grieving process.

- Manage Your Heart: Whether or not the person repents, work on maintaining a clean heart as you grieve. Don't allow unforgiveness, offense, and bitterness to take root in the midst of pain, sadness, and anger.

- Set Boundaries: By refusing to repair connection with you, this person has changed the relationship. If the person tries to negotiate a way to continue the relationship without working out the issues, thus asking you to tolerate continued conflict, set clear and firm limits that communicate that until the repair work is done, you cannot move forward in the relationship.

- Try Again: Let the person know that reconciliation is still on the table when they're ready and willing to work things out.

EXAMINE YOUR FOUNDATION

Have you ever been in a relationship where the other person refused to adjust following a confrontation? If so, how did you handle this?

EXAMINE YOUR FOUNDATION

Is there a broken relationship in your life? What is your heart toward that person?

Core Value

When people fail to resolve conflict and repair connection following a confrontation, honoring responses include forgiveness, setting boundaries, and carrying hope for future repentance and reconciliation.

FOUNDATION STORY: "WHAT PROBLEM?"

I still remember the day I discovered that a friend of mine, who I worked with and supervised in ministry, was involved in a sexually immoral relationship. Though I was shocked and disappointed, I carried hope that she would be repentant and would work on building a solution to this problem. Sadly, when I confronted her, it became clear that she did not think there was a problem. In fact, she had decided that this immoral relationship was the solution to what she perceived as her problem—loneliness—and was willing to sacrifice nearly everything to keep it.

As long as she did not agree that she had made a mess in our environment and refused to clean it up, there could be no reconciliation or restoration for her within our community. Within a few months, she had left her job and community to pursue this relationship. It was heartbreaking.

My friend's decision changed our relationship. We went from having fairly frequent contact and conversations to almost none. My wife, Sheri, reached out to her a few times, but it became clear that she was not interested in initiating contact with us. However, I kept my love toward her and prayed that one day she would have a change of heart. A few years later, it happened. My friend contacted us, explained that she had ended the bad relationship, and began moving towards us again. I'm thankful to say that God has been faithfully restoring her life in beautiful ways.

CULTURAL EFFECTS

STRONGER PEOPLE:

- People receive healing and greater freedom from problematic beliefs and wounds that are keeping them from living as honoring sons and daughters.

- People grow in their ability to be vulnerable, to manage anxiety, to communicate bravely, and to adjust to other people.

STRONGER CONNECTIONS:

- Disconnected relationships are repaired, and the issues that caused the disconnection are resolved.

- People develop improved patterns of behavior and interaction that meet needs more effectively and build intimacy.

RESPONSE TO UNSUCCESSFUL CONFRONTATION:

- Healthy boundaries are set up to prevent continued conflict, even as hope is maintained for the person/people to repent and reconcile.

- The standard of honor is maintained by holding the standard of love, respect, trust, and connection in relationships, even if one or more parties decide to dishonor that standard.

REFLECT & DISCUSS:

Do you see these cultural effects in your relational environment(s)? Explain.

LAY A SOLID FOUNDATION

STUDY

- Stronger People: Luke 7:47

- Stronger Connections: Ephesians 4:14-16

- Response to Unsuccessful Confrontation: Matthew 18:23-35. What is required to forgive your brother "from your heart"?

PRAY

- Invite God to increase your self-understanding, wisdom, and courage to take responsibility for your beliefs, emotions, needs, and how your behavior is affecting people around you.

- Pray that God will enable you to practice successful confrontation in order to grow as a person of honor in honoring relationships.

DO

- Write out a list of personal goals and commitments for practicing successful confrontation in each of the following areas:

  - Feedback:

  - Humility:

  - Identifying Problems:

  - Creating Solutions:

  - Strengthening Connections:

EMPOWERING THE PEOPLE AROUND YOU

SESSION 6

EMPOWERING THE PEOPLE AROUND YOU

FOUNDATION STONE #17: VALUING PEOPLE

> *"But command Joshua, and encourage him and strengthen him; for he shall go over before this people, and he shall cause them to inherit the land which you will see."* DEUTERONOMY 3:28

Communicating and demonstrating value for people empowers them and invites their best to the surface. Three of the primary ways we communicate and demonstrate value are:

1) *Getting to know people* through conversation, observation, and shared experiences, as well as assessments that identify strengths, skills, and behavior styles (e.g., StrengthsFinder, DISC)

2) *Trusting people* with responsibilities that fit their strengths and involve decision-making and influence.

3) *Appreciating people* through encouragement, praise, thanks, and increased trust.

Empowering leaders work to establish a culture in which people feel known, trusted, and appreciated.

EXAMINE YOUR FOUNDATION

Describe an experience in your life that helped you get to know someone really well. What did the experience show you about the person?

Has someone trusted you in a way that made you feel valued? Describe.

What are the systems of affirmation in the various environments in which you live and work? How does the level of appreciation affect you and the people around you?

Core Value

We empower people when we communicate value for them through knowing, trusting, and appreciating them.

FOUNDATION STONE #18: COMMUNICATING VISION

Where there is no vision, the people are unrestrained,
But happy is he who keeps the law. PROVERBS 29:18 NASB

Then the LORD answered me and said:
"Write the vision
And make it plain on tablets,
That he may run who reads it." HABAKKUK 2:2

Vision is empowering. When people see where they are being called and invited to go, they move into action. In order to sustain momentum in pursuing vision, the following elements must be present:

1) Leaders regularly articulate the corporate vision and encourage a culture where the vision is discussed among individuals and teams.

2) Personal vision remains connected to the larger corporate vision.

3) Goal-setting, strategies, plans, and assignments for reaching the vision are developed collaboratively between leaders and followers.

4) Adjustments to goals, plans, or assignments are likewise made collaboratively.

EXAMINE YOUR FOUNDATION

Have you experienced relational environments where vision is lacking or confusing? If so, how did this affect you and others?

How does your personal vision connect to and flow from the corporate vision of the relational environments in which you are most involved?

What do you need from a leader to feel empowered as you fulfill your role in pursuing vision?

Core Value

*In honoring relational environments, vision is communicated clearly,
discussed regularly, and pursued collaboratively.*

FOUNDATION STONE #19: TEAM BUILDING

I want you to get out there and walk—better yet, run!—on the road God called you to travel. I don't want any of you sitting around on your hands. I don't want anyone strolling off, down some path that goes nowhere. And mark that you do this with humility and discipline—not in fits and starts, but steadily, pouring yourselves out for each other in acts of love, alert at noticing differences and quick at mending fences. You were all called to travel on the same road and in the same direction, so stay together, both outwardly and inwardly…Everything you are and think and do is permeated with Oneness. EPHESIANS 4:1-6 MSG

A team is a group of people working together to fulfill a common vision. Members of a team are empowered when they feel valued and trusted, collaborate well with each other, and work in roles suited to their strengths. Empowered teams draw out the best of each team member and function synergistically, thereby accomplishing far more than the individual members could on their own.

Honoring team leaders focus on communicating vision, empowering team members, and facilitating synergistic collaboration. They endeavor to create an environment where team members are invited to be authentic and vulnerable, where they learn to appreciate and work with people whose strengths are different than theirs, and where they feel believed in even when they fail.

EXAMINE YOUR FOUNDATION

Do you feel like your experience working in a team has helped to bring the best of you to the surface? Why or why not?

What are some of the biggest challenges you've encountered to collaborating successfully on a team?

Have the leaders in your life been a "lid" or a "launch pad" for you and the teams you've worked on? Describe the team dynamics fostered by the leaders that you have served.

Core Value

In honoring, relational environments, vision is communicated clearly, discussed regularly, and pursued collaboratively.

FOUNDATION STORY: "JUNGLE SCHOOL BOARD"

When leaders on a team don't know how to honor one another's differences, they often end up accomplishing nothing, much like the animals in the "Jungle School Board" fable published over a hundred years ago:

> When the animals decided to establish schools, they selected a school board consisting of Mr. Elephant, Mr. Kangaroo and Mr. Monkey, and these fellows held a meeting to agree upon their plans.
>
> "What shall the animals' children be taught in the animal school? That is the question," declared Mr. Monkey.
>
> "Yes, that is the question," exclaimed Mr. Kangaroo and Mr. Elephant together.
>
> "They should be taught to climb trees," said the monkey, positively. "All my relatives will serve as teachers."
>
> "No, indeed!" shouted the other two, in chorus. "That would never do."
>
> "They should he taught to jump," cried the kangaroo, with emphasis. "All of my relatives will be glad to teach them."
>
> "No, indeed!" yelled the other two, in unison. "That would never do."
>
> "They should be taught to look wise," said the elephant. "And all of my relatives will act as teachers."

"No, indeed!" howled the other two together. "That will never do."

"Well, what will do?" they asked, as they looked at each other in perplexity.

"Teach them to climb," said Mr. Monkey.

"Teach them to jump," said Mr. Kangaroo.

"Teach them to look wise," said Mr. Elephant.

And so it was that none of them would yield, and when they saw there was no chance to agree, they all became angry and decided not to have any animal schools at all.[3]

Collaboration becomes impossible when leaders can't find the gold in each person's contribution. When we insist on a "one size fits all" approach, we will never build anything—especially anything greater than what any one person is able to conceive or accomplish. Leaders must realize that problems can be solved in many ways, with many tools and approaches. While leading teams, I have often pointed out, "When somebody's good with a hammer, they try to turn everything into a nail."

Along with not insisting that everyone do the same job the same way, we must match people's jobs with their unique strengths, gifts, talents, and design if we want to get the best of them. Albert Einstein sometimes gets credited with the saying, "Everybody is a genius. But if you judge a fish by its ability to climb a tree, it will live its whole life believing that it is stupid."

---

[3] *The Illinois State Journal, For Women and Children:* Jungle School Board, Quote Page 4, Springfield, Illinois, April 29, 1903 (GenealogyBank) (http://quoteinvestigator.com/2013/04/06/fish-climb/, accessed July 30, 2015)

CULTURAL EFFECTS

GETTING TO KNOW PEOPLE:

- People who feel known, trusted, and appreciated are motivated and empowered to offer their best in relationships and roles.

- Productivity increases because leaders know their people, give them appropriate opportunities and responsibilities, and make sure they are thriving.

COMMUNICATING VISION:

- People have a clear understanding of what "success" looks like, which brings focus, value, and momentum to their daily tasks, short-term goals, and long-term plans.

- Relationships, families, teams, and communities are preserved because personal vision and corporate vision are clear and connected.

TEAM BUILDING:

- People grow in their ability to appreciate and develop their own strengths, as well as appreciate and collaborate with team members who have different strengths.

- Anxiety is lowered, while trust and productivity increase, as leaders create a safe place for team members to collaborate.

REFLECT & DISCUSS:

Do you see these cultural effects in your relational environment(s)? Explain.

LAY A SOLID FOUNDATION

STUDY

- Read *StrengthsFinder 2.0* by Tom Rath.

PRAY

- Ask God to help you grow to appreciate what you don't understand about other people's strengths, behavior styles, needs, and gifts.

- Ask for wisdom and humility to empower others to be strong in areas where you are weak.

- Ask for grace to trust God to build His Church in ways you wouldn't, using people who are different and even with whom you disagree.

- Pray that God will enable you to practice successful confrontation in order to grow as a person of honor in honoring relationships.

DO

- Take the DISC or StrengthsFinder assessments online.

- Find a coach to help you apply the results of these assessments.

- Arrange for your team or family members to take the same assessments.

- Build plans to empower your people in their strengths, gifts, and design.

LONG-TERM RELATIONSHIPS

SESSION 7

LONG-TERM RELATIONSHIPS

FOUNDATION STONE #20: THE FRAMEWORK OF FAMILY

> *... I bow my knees to the Father of our Lord Jesus Christ, from whom the whole family in heaven and earth is named...* EPHESIANS 3:14-15
>
> *The way we know we've been transferred from death to life is that we love our brothers and sisters.* I JOHN 3:14 MSG

The phrase, "The Kingdom is modeled after family," is based on the truth that God consists of three related persons—Father, Son, and Holy Spirit—and that He created humanity in this relational image to be a family. The kingdom of God is realized in our lives the more we learn to honor and express God's design for our spiritual family relationships with Him and one another.

Two features of our spiritual family that we must honor in order to think and act from the framework of family are the following:

1) Our spiritual family is permanent and chosen by God. Thus, we are called to love, serve, and forgive one another with eternal consequences in mind.

2) While God is the eternal Father of our family, He passes spiritual inheritance from generation to generation through the relationships of spiritual fathers and mothers to spiritual fathers and sons. The command to "Honor your father and your mother" (Exodus 20:12) still applies. We should carry a value to receive, develop, and pass on a spiritual inheritance to the next generation.

EXAMINE YOUR FOUNDATION

In your family of origin, were family relationships protected and preserved for the long term, or were they broken? How has this experience shaped your understanding of "the framework of family"?

How has entering into a relationship with the Father as a beloved son or daughter shaped your hope and desire to establish healthy relationships that can stand the test of time?

Core Value

We honor the truth that God has chosen us as members of His eternal family by working to preserve and protect long-term relationships.

FOUNDATION STONE #21: REMOVING THE PUNISHER

"You have heard that it was said, 'You shall love your neighbor and hate your enemy.' But I say to you, love your enemies, bless those who curse you, do good to those who hate you, and pray for those who spitefully use you and persecute you, that you may be sons of your Father in heaven…"
MATTHEW 5:43-45

Hatred stirs up strife,
But love covers all sins. PROVERBS 10:12

There is no fear in love. But perfect love drives out fear, because fear has to do with punishment. The one who fears is not made perfect in love. I JOHN 4:18 NIV

Many of us grew up in relational environments where punishment was used to control wrong, hurtful behavior. We learned that when we messed up, people would get angry, withhold love, or find other ways to hold what we had done over our heads so that we would never do it again. Punishment is driven by fear and creates fragile relationships in which the level of trust is low and the level of anxiety is high. Sons and daughters of God, however, are to be driven by love, not fear. Perfect love—love that is complete and without defect—responds to wrong or hurt with truth, humility, vulnerability, and forgiveness rather than punishment and control. Love always seeks to heal connection after it has been damaged, and creates high-trust, low-anxiety relationships. Perfect love—love without punishment—is the essential ingredient for building healthy long-term relationships.

EXAMINE YOUR FOUNDATION

What kinds of responses to hurtful or wrong behavior did you see and/or learn growing up? Which of these responses were forms of control and punishment driven by fear?

EXAMINE YOUR FOUNDATION

How would you describe the level of trust and connection and the level of anxiety in your family relationships growing up? How was this connected to the presence of punishment in the relational dynamics?

_____

_____

_____

_____

How do you respond to those closest to you when you are hurt? Would you say that the "punisher" shows up in your relationships? Why or why or not?

_____

_____

_____

_____

Core Value

In order to build healthy long-term relationships, we must cast out fear, control, and punishment with perfect love.

FOUNDATION STONE #22: FINISHING WELL

Many will say they are loyal friends,
but who can find one who is truly reliable? PROVERBS 20:6 NLT

This is My commandment, that you love one another as I have loved you. Greater love has no one than this, than to lay down one's life for his friends. JOHN 15:12-13

When we get to the end of our lives, the only thing that will matter is whether we were faithful to trust, love, and obey Jesus. And according to Him, His first priority for us is that we love one another as He loved us. Jesus' love for us is faithful, sacrificial, unconditional, and enduring. We simply can't imagine Jesus ever walking away from a relationship. As Paul wrote, "If we are unfaithful, he remains faithful, for he cannot deny who he is" (2 Timothy 2:13 NLT). He is committed to loving us for eternity. This is the standard for us to pursue in our relationships with one another.

In a culture where covenants and relational commitments seem to be more fragile and devalued than ever, it is essential that we look to Jesus as our standard of love and faithfulness. He is the only One with the grace to help us love people well to the end.

EXAMINE YOUR FOUNDATION

At the end of your life, what do you want to be true about the way you loved people in long-term relationships?

EXAMINE YOUR FOUNDATION

Have you reached a point in a relationship where you want to give up on the relationship? What did you do and what was the result?

_____
_____
_____
_____
_____

Do you think about the effects your relational choices will have on the next generation? Why or why not?

_____
_____
_____
_____
_____

Core Value

People of honor commit to following Jesus' standard for faithfully loving people to the end in long-term relationships.

FOUNDATION STORY: "JOHN TILLERY"

Years ago, Sheri and I had a spiritual father in our lives named John Tillery. John was the executive director of a social services company where we worked for nine years. Early on, he selected me as someone he wanted to promote through the company and paid for most of my tuition as I pursued my master's degree in social work.

Then, after nearly a decade of this man investing so completely in our lives, there came the day when Sheri and I met with John and informed him that Bill Johnson had asked me to be his associate pastor in Weaverville, our old hometown. We explained how God had spoken to us and confirmed that He was calling us to this new ministry career.

John looked at us and said, "I consider it an honor to be part of what God is doing in your life. I'm grateful to have contributed anything to help prepare you for what He has for you. I release you from all sense of obligation to this company or to me personally, and I bless you to go into all it is that God has for you."

John was such an example of what it looks like to have a true father, someone who would generously and sacrificially invest in my life for the sake of helping me fulfill God's purpose for me in His kingdom. Every person that Sheri and I have impacted is fruit of John Tillery's investment.

CULTURAL EFFECTS

THE FRAMEWORK OF FAMILY:

- People are more willing and committed to work through conflicts and preserve connection because they see one another as brothers and sisters who are accountable to their Father.

- Spiritual inheritance is passed successfully between spiritual parents and children.

REMOVING THE PUNISHER:

- The root causes of wrong or hurtful behavior can actually be addressed and healed because people choose to speak the truth in love rather than punishing.

- Relational connections grow stronger through resolving conflict when punishment is off the table.

FINISHING WELL:

- People who hold themselves accountable to Jesus' standard of faithfulness access grace to honor that standard and don't give up on relationships.

- People who care about passing a strong relational legacy on to the next generation honor and uphold their covenants.

REFLECT & DISCUSS

Do you see these cultural effects in your relational environment(s)? Explain.

LAY A SOLID FOUNDATION

STUDY

- Recommended Reading: *Keep Your Love On* by Danny Silk

PRAY

- Ask to see the opportunities around you to build into the long-term benefits of others.

- Ask for grace to forgive and bless those who have hurt or scared you.

- Ask for the ability to see what God is doing in the lives of those who touch your life.

DO

- Renew your covenant character to keep your love on no matter what.

- Continually build your communication skills.

- Learn to set healthy, life-giving boundaries with your priorities and vital relationships.

EXPORTING HONOR

SESSION 8

EXPORTING HONOR

FOUNDATION STONE #23: REMOVING "US" AND "THEM"

> *But now in Christ Jesus you who once were far away have been brought near by the blood of Christ. For he himself is our peace, who has made the two groups one and has destroyed the barrier, the dividing wall of hostility, by setting aside in his flesh the law with its commands and regulations. His purpose was to create in himself one new humanity out of the two, thus making peace, and in one body to reconcile both of them to God through the cross, by which he put to death their hostility.*
> EPHESIANS 2:13-16 NIV
>
> *For Christ's love compels us, because we are convinced that one died for all, and therefore all died. And he died for all, that those who live should no longer live for themselves but for him who died for them and was raised again. So from now on we regard no one from a worldly point of view.*
> 2 CORINTHIANS 5:14-16 NIV

The divisions between "us" and "them" in the Church today align more with the Old Testament paradigm that defines people's spirituality according to what they do. This paradigm makes church leaders the most spiritual, churchgoers less spiritual, and nonbelievers least spiritual. In contrast, the New Testament defines our spirituality according to what Christ has done. The closer we get to Him, the more we see people through the lens of the finished work of the cross, which forever removed every dividing wall created by sin. In this paradigm, the more spiritual we become, the more we carry Christ's heart to embrace all people and repair all separation between us. We also honor the fact that the "work of ministry" is to be carried out by all the saints, not just church leaders, in whatever position or role God calls them to in society (see Ephesians 4:12).

EXAMINE YOUR FOUNDATION

What are some expressions of an "us and them" paradigm you have encountered within the Church?

Do you struggle to believe that some people have more spiritual callings than others? Why or why not?

Core Value

The finished work of the cross removes divisions and false spiritual hierarchies, and compels us to honor and embrace all those for whom Christ died.

FOUNDATION STONE #24: LOVING THROUGH SERVICE

> *Jesus called them together and said, "You know that the rulers of the Gentiles lord it over them, and their high officials exercise authority over them. Not so with you. Instead, whoever wants to become great among you must be your servant, and whoever wants to be first must be your slave—just as the Son of Man did not come to be served, but to serve, and to give his life as a ransom for many."*
> MATTHEW 25:25-28 NIV

When Jesus served people, He wasn't serving their agenda, but He was meeting their needs, and He was doing it solely for their benefit. This is the model of service to which He calls us. In order to serve our communities, cities, nation, and the world effectively, we need to pursue the following qualities:

1) Ownership—taking responsibility for the welfare of our communities.

2) Compassion—opening our hearts to the needs of those around us.

3) Wisdom—seeking to bring God's design for human flourishing into the places where we are serving and communicating it effectively so that it can be received.

4) Humility—listening and responding to the felt needs of those we are serving and honoring the service and contributions of others.

EXAMINE YOUR FOUNDATION

Where has God called you to serve in your community, and what are the biggest needs you see there?

EXAMINE YOUR FOUNDATION

Has God given you insights and strategies for how to express the wisdom of the Kingdom where you are serving? If so, what are they?

_____
_____
_____
_____
_____

What are some of the biggest challenges believers face in serving in their communities?

_____
_____
_____
_____
_____

Core Value

We export honor to our communities through service marked by ownership, humility, compassion, and wisdom.

FOUNDATION STONE #24: POSITIONED FOR INFLUENCE

"You are the salt of the earth; but if the salt loses its flavor, how shall it be seasoned? It is then good for nothing but to be thrown out and trampled underfoot by men. You are the light of the world. A city that is set on a hill cannot be hidden. Nor do they light a lamp and put it under a basket, but on a lampstand, and it gives light to all who are in the house. Let your light so shine before men, that they may see your good works and glorify your Father in heaven." MATTHEW 5:13-16

Jesus made it clear that we were to have visible, tangible influence in the lives of those around us. That influence can be stopped, however, if we lose our "flavor"—that is, become like the world around us—or hide ourselves from view. In order for the people of God to have and maintain influence, we must commit to being who we are in Him without compromise, and we must be courageous in letting people see who we are through "good works." This term "good" (Greek: *kalos*) means "beautiful, excellent, useful, precious, admirable, noble, honorable, or conferring honor."[4] As we serve in ways that contribute the beauty, excellence, nobility, and honor of the Kingdom to our communities, we will create an environment where people see and give honor to our Father. This exchange of honor makes a way for greater influence.

EXAMINE YOUR FOUNDATION

What are some examples of beautiful, excellent, noble, useful, and honorable things Christians have contributed to the world?

Do you see areas where the Church may be either compromising her distinctiveness in the world or trying to hide from the world? If so, what are they?

[4] See Strong's G2570

EXAMINE YOUR FOUNDATION

What is necessary for you personally to fulfill Jesus' command to be a tangible, visible influence to those around you?

Core Value

We are responsible to tangibly, visibly influence the world around us through good works that put the beauty, excellence, nobility, and honor of the Kingdom on display.

FOUNDATION STORY: "ADVANCE REDDING"

When Advance Redding, a nonprofit organization founded by Bethel Church, took over the lease of the Redding Civic Auditorium, many city officials and organizations expressed their concern and anxiety over the idea of a religious community managing this beloved facility. However, through consistently demonstrating wisdom, excellence, compassion, and service, Advance Redding, led by my wife Sheri, grew to be highly respected, valuable, and trusted by city leaders.

Advance Redding's mission was simple. They wanted to raise the experience of everyone who rented the Civic Auditorium to the level of *excellent*. Many people were apparently surprised to discover that Advance Redding had no other agenda than to serve those using the facility. Many city officials and representatives from businesses and nonprofit organizations ended up confessing to Sheri that they had expected to be limited, censored, and judged by the Advance Redding team. Instead, they were shocked to discover that the service of Advance Redding enabled them to be more excellent and efficient in the way they set up their functions, thereby increasing revenues and expanding their capacity to accomplish their mission. Their experience led them to see Advance Redding as an ally, an advocate, and an advisor.

Memorably, one City of Redding council member told Sheri, "You are the perfect person to bridge Bethel Church and the City of Redding. It was so surprising to find out that you were normal."

Christians truly can be normal, loving people when they're not trying to manipulate people or impose a religious agenda on the community. When we get out of our own way and embrace the people around us, we put Jesus on display. Believe it or not, Jesus is normal!

CULTURAL EFFECTS

REMOVING "US" AND "THEM":

- False pressure to be more "spiritual" than those they are leading is lifted off of church leaders.

- Instead of remaining dependent on a small number of spiritual elites, believers are equipped and challenged to become mature ministers of the Gospel in their daily lives.

LOVING THROUGH SERVICE:

- As needs are met and Kingdom wisdom filters into a community, every aspect of society begins to flourish.

- Service opens the door to trusting relationships with people in a community.

POSITIONED FOR INFLUENCE:

- The Church gains a reputation for being those who contribute beauty, excellence, nobility, and honor to the community.

- People see and are attracted to the Father as they taste and see the goodness in the lives of His sons and daughters.

REFLECT & DISCUSS:

Do you see these cultural effects in your relational environment(s)? Explain.

LAY A SOLID FOUNDATION

STUDY

- Recommended Listening: "Dreams of Kings" by Danny Silk, available at the Bethel Store: https://shop.ibethel.org/products/dreams-of-kings.

PRAY

Ask the Lord for:

- Wisdom and compassion.

- Revelation of strategies for your city.

- Grace for your city to see a loving Father.

DO

- Find community leaders to serve with your gifts and resources.

- Bring good news to civic leaders. Show up at city and county board meetings with testimonies of progress or benefits the city is experiencing. Be verbally thankful towards civil servants.

- Meet with city leaders to find out the areas of need that are important to them. Target those areas for success. Aim to make city leaders look like geniuses.

BUILDING SUCCESSION MOMENTUM

SESSION 9

BUILDING SUCCESSION MOMENTUM

FOUNDATION STONE #26: MISSION AND METHOD

And Jesus came and spoke to them, saying, "All authority has been given to Me in heaven and on earth. Go therefore and make disciples of all the nations, baptizing them in the name of the Father and of the Son and of the Holy Spirit, teaching them to observe all things that I have commanded you; and lo, I am with you always, even to the end of the age." MATTHEW 28:18-20

For as many as are led by the Spirit of God, these are sons of God. ROMANS 8:14

It is truly astounding that in three years, Jesus prepared twelve men to take the baton from Him and lead the next generation in carrying out His mission on the earth. Yet Jesus clearly commanded and expected every generation of His disciples—including us—to imitate His model for succession, which consisted of fulfilling the following mission through the following method:

- Mission: To restore sons and daughters to the Father, teach them to walk by the Spirit, and commission them to call other lost sons and daughters back to the Father.

- Method: Reveal the Father in the context of a long-term relationship by demonstrating the power and priorities of His Kingdom and modeling what it looks like to live in complete unity and dependence on the Holy Spirit.

EXAMINE YOUR FOUNDATION

How have spiritual leaders in your life demonstrated—or failed to demonstrate—a value for the presence of God and dependence on the Holy Spirit?

How are you pursuing a lifestyle of dependence on the Spirit, and how are you demonstrating this to those around you?

Why are long-term relationships essential to discipleship?

Core Value

We transfer Jesus' mission successfully to the next generation by cultivating relationships in which we train people to be led by the Spirit and walk in His power and presence.

FOUNDATION STONE #27: TRAINING THROUGH RELATIONSHIP

> *My dear child, don't shrug off God's discipline, but don't be crushed by it either. It's the child he loves that he disciplines; the child he embraces, he also corrects. God is educating you; that's why you must never drop out. He's treating you as dear children. This trouble you're in isn't punishment; it's training, the normal experience of children. Only irresponsible parents leave children to fend for themselves. Would you prefer an irresponsible God? We respect our own parents for training and not spoiling us, so why not embrace God's training so we can truly live? While we were children, our parents did what seemed best to them. But God is doing what is best for us, training us to live God's holy best. At the time, discipline isn't much fun. It always feels like it's going against the grain. Later, of course, it pays off handsomely, for it's the well-trained who find themselves mature in their relationship with God.* HEBREWS 12:5-11 MSG

Jesus modeled the type of relationship that enables spiritual parents to successfully reproduce themselves and cultivate spiritual maturity in their children. The following elements are essential to this relationship:

1) Proximity: Jesus took the disciples wherever He went and let them watch and participate in everything He did.

2) Interaction: Jesus invited questions and asked provoking questions to get the disciples to examine and change their thinking. He created a safe place for them to learn.

3) Empowerment: Jesus communicated value, trust, and affirmation to His disciples with clear, targeted words about their identity, purpose, and calling in Him.

Each of these elements communicates the honoring message, "I value you, and I believe in you," to a spiritual son or daughter, and calls them to return that honor by paying the price to grow, mature, and invest in the next generation.

EXAMINE YOUR FOUNDATION

Who are the spiritual parents who have invested gifts of time, proximity, challenging interaction, and empowerment in your life, and how have they done so?

_____

_____

_____

_____

_____

What are some provoking questions that leaders in your life have asked you, and how have they changed your thinking and life?

_____

_____

_____

_____

_____

Core Value

Spiritual parents honor their spiritual sons and daughters by investing the time, challenging interaction, and encouraging words necessary to cultivate spiritual maturity in them.

FOUNDATION STONE #28: TRAINING THROUGH RELATIONSHIP

Keep your eyes on Jesus, who both began and finished this race we're in. Study how he did it. Because he never lost sight of where he was headed—that exhilarating finish in and with God—he could put up with anything along the way: Cross, shame, whatever. And now he's there, in the place of honor, right alongside God. When you find yourselves flagging in your faith, go over that story again, item by item, that long litany of hostility he plowed through. That will shoot adrenaline into your souls!
HEBREWS 12:2-3 MSG

Every good succession plan must impart keys to longevity. Good spiritual fathers and mothers want their sons and daughters to run their race to the end and finish well, and one of the most important ways they do this is by informing and managing their expectations regarding the timeline and principles of God's process of maturity in their lives. The following principles are essential for the next generation to embrace if they want to train for endurance:

1) God's timeline is usually much longer than what we imagine.

2) Every promotion means an increased weight of responsibility. If we seek promotion before we have the strength and skill to handle it, it will crush us.

3) The best, safest promotion comes in the context of community and fathering.

Each of these keys to longevity works through honor. Honoring God's timeline, His process to prepare us for increased responsibility, and the leaders He has placed over us sets us up to run with endurance.

EXAMINE YOUR FOUNDATION

Have you ever gotten frustrated with where you are in life because you felt you were behind or God was slow? How did you adjust your expectations regarding God's timeline in your life?

Who is someone in your life who models perseverance in their walk with God?

Core Value

Spiritual fathers and mothers train the next generation to run with endurance by teaching them to honor God's timeline and process of maturity.

FOUNDATION STORY: "TAYLOR'S NAME BADGE"

Years ago, my youngest son, Taylor, used to hang out at Bethel Church during conferences and come and go from meetings as he pleased. Eventually, however, the conference planners become stricter about who could enter the sanctuary and who couldn't. They instituted that every conference attendee had to wear a name badge, and staff members stood at the door to inspect the name badges and only allow those with a badge to attend the meetings.

One day, a conference staff person stopped Taylor at the sanctuary door as he tried to enter and told him, "I'm sorry, but you can't come in without a name badge."

Taylor couldn't believe it, but instead of trying to argue with the staff person, he turned around and headed for my office. I was not there when he arrived, but sitting on my desk was my own name badge reading, "Danny Silk." Taylor took the badge, grabbed a pen, and made a few quick changes to it. When he returned to the sanctuary door, he was wearing a name badge that proclaimed, "Danny Silk's Son."

Taylor started wearing that name badge around so that everybody knew that he was connected to somebody greater than himself—and so that he could get through the doors he couldn't get through on his own.

CULTURAL EFFECTS

MISSION AND METHOD:

- Leaders who model a value for the power and presence of the Holy Spirit create true followers of God, not of themselves.

- People bear supernatural fruit through intimacy with the Holy Spirit rather than human striving.

TRAINING THROUGH RELATIONSHIPS:

- Leaders who invest in people and truly impart who they are can trust their sons and daughters to represent their heart and mission accurately.

- Spiritual sons and daughters who are loved, believed in, and served by their leaders will imitate this model with the next generation.

TRAINING FOR ENDURANCE:

- Sons and daughters don't get as anxious or frustrated in God's process and don't fall prey to the temptation of acting outside it.

- Promotion is blessed because sons and daughters wait for God's and their leaders' permission and support to step into greater responsibility.

REFLECT & DISCUSS:

Do you see these cultural effects in your relational environment(s)? Explain.

LAY A SOLID FOUNDATION

STUDY

- Recommended Listening: "The Successive Covenant" by Danny Silk, available online at the Bethel Store: https://shop.ibethel.org/products/the-successive-covenant-6-00pm-october-20-2013.

- Recommended Reading: *Loving Our Kids On Purpose* by Danny Silk.

PRAY

- Ask for increased grace and wisdom to know the Father and be led by the Spirit, so this will be what you model to the next generation.

- Ask for more love, courage, and patience as you give spiritual sons and daughters access to your life and invest in their lives.

- Ask the Holy Spirit for words of encouragement, exhortation, and comfort to build up your spiritual sons and daughters.

DO

- If you don't have them already, ask the Lord to show you who you are to be investing in as a spiritual father or mother and build a relationship with them. Teach, equip, and empower them to know the Father and be led by the Spirit.

LAYING THE FOUNDATION OF HONOR

SESSION 10

LAYING THE FOUNDATION OF HONOR

Congratulations! You have nearly completed this journey of digging deeply into the biblical core values that comprise the Foundations of Honor in a relational environment. You have also hopefully begun to engage with the recommendations at the end of each session for how you can further study and practically apply these core values in your life, family, business, school, church, or organization.

This final session is an invitation to make an individual and corporate commitment to upholding the core values of honor in the form of a social agreement, or Constitution of Honor.

Please read the following template for a Constitution of Honor:

CONSTITUTION OF HONOR
Core Values and Commitments

WHAT IS HONOR?

1. Honor calls people to *perfect freedom*—the ability to express the Father's design for our relationships and reproduce His kingdom of love.

   - Commitment: *We will be powerful in using our freedom to love God and others.*

2. Honor involves valuing, building, and protecting relationships.

    • Commitment: *We will develop the skills and attitudes necessary to build and protect healthy relational connections.*

3. Honor connects our individual destinies to our common purpose: "On earth as it is in heaven."

    • Commitment: *We will continually seek to align our hearts, minds, and behavior with heaven so that we accurately appreciate people's unique destinies and how they work together.*

CULTIVATING AN ABUNDANCE MINDSET

4. People of honor carry an abundance mindset based in the Father's heart to supply every son and daughter with the resources, opportunities, and wisdom to flourish, succeed, and overflow with blessing to others.

    • Commitment: *We will seek to approach our lives and those around us with an expectation that there is always enough to fulfill our divine calling and assignments.*

5. While the resources of the Father's house are unlimited, they flow to and through us as we become fully aligned with His heart and His mission and with the leaders He has called to equip us to fulfill that mission.

    • Commitment: *We will align ourselves with the godly leaders in our lives and their mission as they align with Christ.*

6. Generosity is an essential joy, privilege, and responsibility for people of honor.

    • Commitment: *We will establish a lifestyle of extravagant generosity through cheerfully giving and investing in people.*

CONFRONTATION

7. People of honor are prepared to confront behavior that threatens the health of relational connections.

   - Commitment: *We will refuse to allow the fear of confrontation to infect our relational connections.*

8. People of honor highly value giving and receiving feedback to create awareness of how others are experiencing us, and we are experiencing others.

   - Commitment: *We will call out the best in people and trust others to call out the best in us.*

9. People of honor create a safe place to give and receive feedback.

   - Commitment: *We will develop the skills to reduce anxiety and give people what they need to experience a safe place as we communicate truth and productive feedback.*

10. People of honor care about meeting the needs of the other person in the relationship and will adjust in order to do so.

    - Commitment: *We will seek to understand the needs of those with whom we are in relationship and be prepared to adjust to meet those needs.*

11. People of honor walk in humility. Humility is essential to successful confrontation.

    - Commitment: *We will esteem and serve one another, especially in confrontations.*

12. Asking good questions in a confrontation creates a safe place to find the core problem(s) needing resolution.

    - Commitment: *We will develop the skills to ask powerful, compassionate questions that help people see and identify the root causes of problematic behavior.*

13. The best person to fix a problem is its owner. Confrontation empowers people to own their problems and collaborate in creating powerful solutions to them.

    - Commitment: *We will empower people to build effective solutions to their own problems and champion them as they carry them out.*

14. A successful confrontation enables people to grow in vulnerability, self-awareness, wisdom, love, courage, freedom, and commitment to honor.

  - Commitment: *We will acknowledge and celebrate the courage it takes to have a successful confrontation and affirm the personal growth that results from it.*

15. A successful confrontation strengthens relational connections by resolving harmful conflict and identifying ways to meet people's needs more effectively.

  - Commitment: *We will learn and practice effective communication skills as our way of life together.*

16. When people fail to resolve conflict and repair connection following a confrontation, honoring responses include forgiveness, setting boundaries, and carrying hope for future repentance and reconciliation.

  - Commitment: *If people fail to resolve a conflict, we will live out forgiveness, set limits as necessary, and always carry hope for the future reconciliation.*

EMPOWERING OTHERS

17. We empower people when we communicate value for them through knowing, trusting, and appreciating them.

  - Commitment: *We will pursue knowledge of people's unique strengths, behavior styles, and other traits so we can entrust them with roles and responsibilities where they can flourish and excel.*

18. In honoring relational environments, vision is communicated clearly, discussed regularly, and pursued collaboratively.

  - Commitment: *We will consistently communicate, discuss, pursue, and partner in our corporate vision.*

19. Honor empowers team members to bring their best to the surface, collaborate successfully, and synergize in pursuing a common vision.

  - Commitment: *We will continually seek to understand, appreciate, and empower the unique contribution of each team member.*

LONG-TERM RELATIONSHIPS

20. We honor the truth that God has chosen us as members of His eternal family by working to preserve and protect long-term relationships.

    - Commitment: *We will remember that we are brothers and sisters and are accountable to the same Father.*

21. In order to build healthy long-term relationships, we must cast out fear, control, and punishment with perfect love.

    - Commitment: *We will respond to hurtful behavior with love and forgiveness rather than fear and punishment.*

22. People of honor commit to following Jesus' standard for faithfully loving people to the end in long-term relationships.

    - Commitment: *We will keep Jesus as our standard and model for loving people faithfully in long-term relationships.*

EXPORTING HONOR

23. The finished work of the cross removes divisions and false spiritual hierarchies, and compels us to honor and embrace all those for whom Christ died.

    - Commitment: *We will remove "us and them" attitudes and agendas in all of our relationships.*

24. We export honor to our communities through service marked by ownership, humility, compassion, and wisdom.

    - Commitment: *We will live as community members and not simply church members.*

25. We are responsible to tangibly, visibly influence the world around us through good works that put the beauty, excellence, nobility, and honor of the Kingdom on display.

    - Commitment: *We will continually look for ways to help people in our community experience the benefits and culture of the Kingdom of Heaven.*

SUCCESSION

26. We transfer Jesus' mission successfully to the next generation by cultivating relationships in which we train people to be led by the Spirit and walk in His power and presence.

    • Commitment: *We will demonstrate the priority of the presence of God to those we lead.*

27. Spiritual parents honor their spiritual sons and daughters by investing the time, challenging interaction, and encouraging words necessary to cultivate spiritual maturity in them.

    • Commitment: *We will raise up leaders from the younger generation in purpose and love.*

28. Spiritual fathers and mothers train the next generation to run with endurance by teaching them to honor God's timeline and process of maturity.

    • Commitment: *We will teach our children the value of inheritance and how to steward it well.*

Next, in order to make this Constitution of Honor your own, take some time to engage more deeply with the commitments listed above by 1) putting them in your own words, and 2) describing some ways these commitments should play out in your life and relationships.

WHAT IS HONOR?

1. *We will be powerful in using our freedom to love God and others.*

> In your own words...

> What does it look like?

2. *We will pursue and develop the skills and attitudes necessary to build and protect healthy relational connections.*

> In your own words...

> What does it look like?

3. *We will continually seek to align our hearts, minds, and behavior with heaven so that we accurately appreciate people's unique destinies and how they work together.*

In your own words…

What does it look like?

CULTIVATING AN ABUNDANCE MINDSET

4. *We will seek to approach our lives and those around us with an expectation that there is always enough to fulfill our divine calling and assignments.*

In your own words…

What does it look like?

5. *We will align ourselves with the godly leaders in our lives and their mission as they align with Christ.*

       In your own words…

       What does it look like?

6. *We will establish a lifestyle of extravagant generosity through cheerfully giving and investing in people.*

       In your own words…

       What does it look like?

CONFRONTATION

7. *We will refuse to allow the fear of confrontation to infect our relational connections.*

In your own words…

What does it look like?

8. *We will call out the best in people and trust others to call out the best in us.*

In your own words…

What does it look like?

9. *We will develop the skills to reduce anxiety and give people what they need to experience a safe place as we communicate truth and productive feedback.*

    In your own words…

    What does it look like?

10. *We will seek to understand the needs of those with whom we are in relationship and be prepared to adjust to meet those needs.*

    In your own words…

    What does it look like?

11. *We will esteem and serve one another, especially in confrontations.*

    In your own words…

    What does it look like?

12. *We will develop the skills to ask powerful, compassionate questions that help people see and identify the root causes of problematic behavior.*

    In your own words…

    What does it look like?

13. *We will empower people to build effective solutions to their own problems and champion them as they carry them out.*

      In your own words…

      What does it look like?

14. *We will acknowledge and celebrate the courage it takes to have a successful confrontation and affirm the personal growth that results from it.*

      In your own words…

      What does it look like?

15. *We will learn and practice effective communication skills as our way of life together.*

In your own words…

What does it look like?

16. *If people fail to resolve a conflict, we will live out forgiveness, set limits as necessary, and always carry hope for future reconciliation.*

In your own words…

What does it look like?

EMPOWERING OTHERS

17. *We will pursue knowledge of people's unique strengths, behavior styles, and other traits so that we can entrust them with roles and responsibilities where they can flourish and excel.*

In your own words…

What does it look like?

18. *We will consistently communicate, discuss, pursue, and partner in our corporate vision.*

In your own words…

What does it look like?

19. *We will continually seek to understand, appreciate, and empower the unique contribution of each team member.*

    In your own words…

    What does it look like?

LONG-TERM RELATIONSHIPS

20. *We will remember that we are brothers and sisters and are accountable to the same Father.*

    In your own words…

    What does it look like?

21. *We will respond to hurtful behavior with love and forgiveness rather than fear and punishment.*

In your own words…

What does it look like?

22. *We will keep Jesus as our standard and model for loving people faithfully in long-term relationships.*

In your own words…

What does it look like?

EXPORTING HONOR

23. *We will remove "us and them" attitudes and agendas in all of our relationships.*

    In your own words...

    What does it look like?

24. *We will live as community members and not simply church members.*

    In your own words...

    What does it look like?

25. *We will continually look for ways to help people in our community experience the benefits and culture of the Kingdom of Heaven.*

        In your own words…

        What does it look like?

SUCCESSION

26. *We will demonstrate the priority of the presence of God to those we lead.*

        In your own words…

        What does it look like?

27. *We will raise up leaders from the younger generation in purpose and love.*

In your own words…

What does it look like?

28. *We will teach our children the value of inheritance and how to steward it well.*

In your own words…

What does it look like?

CONCLUSION

Thank you again for taking this journey through Foundations of Honor. May God empower you with His abundant grace to uphold the core values and commitments of honor. May your life and relationships demonstrate the Father's heart for all people to experience perfect freedom, abundance, healthy confrontation, empowerment, synergistic collaboration, and the benefits of a generational inheritance. May God establish the relational culture of Heaven in and through you, showing the world the beautiful, powerful way in which He created and redeemed us to live and love.

APPENDIX

SUCCESSFUL CONFRONTATION CHECKLIST

PRIOR TO A CONFRONTATION:

1) Check your mind and heart by asking yourself these questions:

   a. Do I have someone who is keeping me accountable through this confrontation process?

   b. Am I entering this confrontation ready to:

      i. Serve and love this person?

      ii. Listen well to identify needs?

      iii. Adjust to meet needs and heal connection?

DURING A CONFRONTATION:

1) Pray and invite the Holy Spirit to come.

2) Declare the goal of the confrontation—to resolve issues that are threatening relational connections and to heal and strengthen those connections. No one is being punished.

3)   Ask the following questions (memorize these!). Use reflective listening to gain mutual understanding of the answers to these questions:

    a. What is the problem?

    b. Who's been affected by that problem?

    c. What will I/you/we do to clean up this mess?

    d. Do you want my help? Who's going to help you/me in this process?

    e. When will the agreed upon steps be completed?

4) Check the emotional "temperature" to make sure everyone is feeling safe, respected, and empowered.

FOLLOWING A CONFRONTATION:

1) Was the confrontation successful in:

    a. Creating a safe place?

    b. Finding the problem(s) and its owner(s)?

    c. Empowering people to develop solutions to the problem(s)?

2) Was the confrontation unsuccessful, and if so, how?

3) What are your personal commitments moving forward from this confrontation?

FEATURED LEADERS

Get to know the leaders in the Foundations of Honor Teaching Series! Further information and resources from each leader may be found on their personal websites and at the Bethel Store.

ERIC JOHNSON

Husband, Dad, Speaker, Author. Co-leads Bethel Redding along with his wife Candace. Prefers to be outside most of the time and always desires to have dessert before dinner.

CANDACE JOHNSON

Candace Johnson co-leads with her husband, Eric, in pastoring Bethel Redding. Her primary focus is creating community that unlocks people and launches them into their destiny. She is passionate about living life to the fullest, setting the captives free, adventure, laughing, being tenderized by God's love, and aiming it at those around her. Captivated by her lovely two daughters and incredible husband, her family makes her feel like the wealthiest person alive!

Product: Eric's book *Christ in You* (Amazon, Bethel Store)

PAUL MANWARING

Paul Manwaring is on the senior leadership team at Bethel Church in Redding, California, and oversees Global Legacy, Bethel's apostolic relational network. He lives to see the secular-sacred dividing line erased in lives and organizations. Paul spent 19 years in senior prison management in England, is a registered general and psychiatric nurse, and holds a management degree from Cambridge University. He is married and has two sons and two grandsons.

Product: *What on Earth Is Glory?*, *Kisses from a Good God* (Amazon, Bethel Store)

DANN FARRELLY

Dann Farrelly is happily married to Christie and they joyfully raise their kids: Adien, Macy and Trace. He has been on staff at Bethel Church in Redding, CA since 1991 and serves on the Local Church and the Senior Leadership Team and is the Dean of Bethel School of Supernatural Ministry. Dann has an M. Div. from Fuller Seminary and teaches preaching, bible, theology and communication with his accessible style and off-beat sense of humor (Which is code for "He thinks he's funny"). He also enjoys sports and writing short bios of himself.

Product: *Brave Communication* (Bethel Store)

STEPHEN DE SILVA

Stephen K. De Silva, founder of Prosperous Soul Ministries and Chief Financial Officer of Bethel Church in Redding, California, has committed his life to breaking the spirits of poverty and mammon and releasing people into their God-given destiny. His unique voice on stewardship and money is a regular part of Bethel Church's adult education, and in seminar form in locations around the globe.

Stephen enjoys life with his wife, Dawna De Silva, founder and co-leader of the international healing and deliverance ministry, Bethel Sozo. Stephen and Dawna have two sons, Timothy and Cory.

Product: *Money* and the *Prosperous Soul* (Amazon, Bethel Store)

SHERI SILK

Sheri currently serves on the Senior Leadership Team of Jesus Culture. Previously, she and Danny served on the Senior Leadership Team of Bethel Church for more than thirteen years. Sheri was also the General Manager of the Redding Civic Auditorium, serving the Redding community while managing events such as conferences and concerts. She and Danny have been married for thirty years, and have three adult children and three grandchildren.

Product: Lovingonpurpose.com

LAUREN VALLOTTON

Lauren Vallotton and her husband, Jason, are the Pastoral Care Overseers at Bethel Church in Redding, California, where they live with their three children. Together, Lauren and Jason are passionate about creating families and cultures of emotional health, freedom, and wholeness! Lauren also enjoys traveling, writing and working with Bethel.TV to see the Kingdom of Heaven advanced into the nations through media! www.laurenvallotton.com

ANDY MASON

Andy Mason comes from New Zealand and has over fifteen years experience in helping individuals and organizations discover and align with purpose, then develop practical steps to make dreams a reality. He has worked for a national consultancy firm and leading financial institution as well as investing in international community development. Andy is the director of Heaven in Business (HeaveninBusiness. com) and recently authored God With You At Work. Andy and his wife, Janine, are the directors of Dream Culture, a movement catalyzing people to discover and live their dreams (iDreamCulture.com). Together they authored Dream Culture: Bringing Dreams to Life. Andy and Janine live with their four children in Redding, California.

Product: *God With You At Work* (Amazon, Bethel Store)

ABI STUMVOLL

When Abi Stumvoll was 12 years old she prayed, "If You can teach me how to love myself, I will change the world." Since that prayer she has gone on a wild journey of divine encounters, purposeful relationships, and breakthrough revelations about the power of love. Abi now teaches others how to walk practically into breakthrough, joy, and the fullness of freedom. She is known for communicating with raw honesty, openness, and hilarious stories.

Abi and her husband, Justin, are madly in love and live in Northern California. They work together in their life consulting business, bringing emotional healing and life transformation to their clients. They also both speak and teach in many different arenas—from classroom environments to conferences and church settings.

Product: Audio teaching (Bethel Store)

TOM CRANDALL

Tom Crandall is the Youth Pastor of Awakening, the youth ministry of Bethel Church in Redding, CA. He and his wife Leslie have served together in full-time youth ministry for over twelve years. They have two amazing children, Joel and Adelyn, and a yellow lab named Bailey. Tom's passion is to see a generation encounter God, discover their identity and purpose, and be empowered to demonstrate the Kingdom in power and love to a lost world.

Product: Audio teaching (Bethel Store)

SETH DAHL

Seth is the Children's Pastor at Bethel Church. His passion is to bring God's Kingdom with signs and wonders, connecting children to the Father's heart so that they will serve Him all the days of their lives. He loves to train up leaders to become spiritually healthy and equip them to bring revival to their ministries.

Seth spent four years working with Metro Ministries in New York City, a ministry that uses over 55 buses to reach 20,000 children each week. Seth and his wife, Lauren, are graduates of BSSM and are enjoying raising their two children, Brooklyn and August. www.sethdahl.com

Product: *ABCDs Of Prophecy Curriculum* (Bethel Store)

BOB HASSON

Bob Hasson is CEO of R.M. Hasson, Inc. and Co-Founder of Lifestreams Ministries. As an entrepreneur and businessman for over thirty-five years, Bob has a heart for leaders of organizations. His passion is to strengthen leaders in all aspects of their organizations focusing on structure, fiscal responsibility and health, and the building of dynamic relationships within the leadership team. For the past thirty years, he has been actively involved in facilitating groups, mentoring leadership teams, and serving on church, ministry, and school boards. As a mediation expert, he is able to help resolve core issues, fostering restoration and vitality in key relationships. He has been married for twenty-seven years to his wife Lauren, and is the proud father of David and his wife, Natthanit, Kyler, Isabella, and Sophia.

Loving On Purpose

Other Loving on Purpose Resources

Love is a choice.
Learn to love on purpose at
lovingonpurpose.com

WHAT IS HONOR AND HOW DO YOU PRACTICE IT?

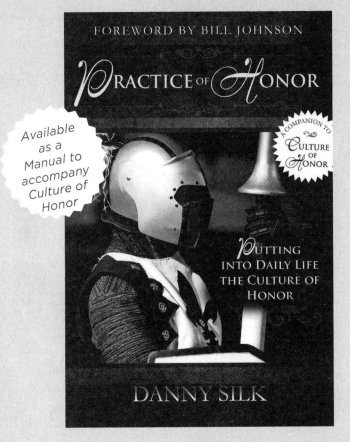

The *Practice of Honor* manual is a practical resource for those who have read *Culture of Honor* by Danny Silk and for leaders, individuals, or those who desire to learn how to cultivate a culture of honor in their sphere of influence. Based on the revival culture of Bethel Church in Redding, California, it is a template to help any leader develop an environment that brings out the very best in people. It is a recipe for introducing the Spirit of God—His freedom—and how to host and embrace that freedom as a community of believers.

View this and more at lovingonpurpose.com

A FRESH, FREEDOM-BASED PERSPECTIVE ON PARENTING

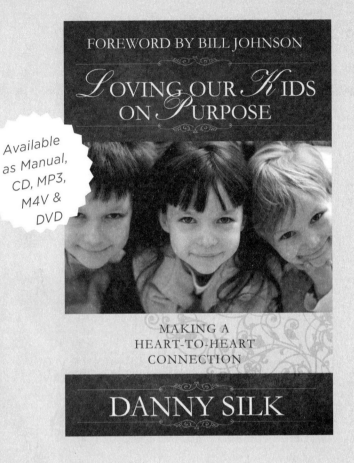

Loving Our Kids On Purpose brings fresh perspective to the age-old role of parenting. Through teaching, storytelling and humor, Danny shares his personal family stories as well as numerous experiences he's had helping other families. You will learn to:

- Protect your heart-to-heart connection with your children
- Teach your children to manage increasing levels of freedom
- Replace the tools of intimidation and control
- Create a safe place for children to build confidence and personal responsibility

View this and more at lovingonpurpose.com

READY FOR MARRIAGE? DANNY EQUIPS YOU FOR THE "BIG" CONVERSATION

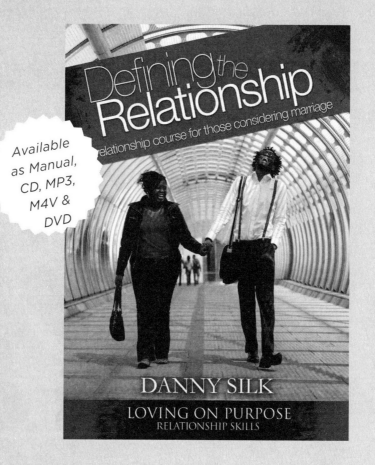

Many Christian couples come to a point where they must "Define their Relationship." In this series, Danny's comedic style of teaching will inspire, challenge, and bring couples into a serious reality check about their decision toward marriage. The goal of this series is to impart COURAGE—the courage to either push through the rugged realities of a loving relationship or the courage to walk away. Whether you are single, dating, or already engaged, this course will teach you how to love on purpose.

View this and more at lovingonpurpose.com